THE STORY OF
NO DOUBT

W9-BAH-270

Copyright © 1997 Omnibus Press
(A Division of Book Sales Limited)

Written by Kalen Rogers
Designed by Amy MacIntyre

Chief Consultant: Emma Edwards

US ISBN 0.8256.1383.3
UK ISBN 0.7119.3864.4
Order No. OP 47576

EXCLUSIVE DISTRIBUTORS:

BOOK SALES LIMITED
8/9 Frith Street, London W1V 5TZ, UK.

MUSIC SALES CORPORATION
257 Park Avenue South, New York, NY 10010, USA.

MUSIC SALES PTY LTD.
120 Rothschild Avenue, Rosebery, NSW 2018, Australia.

To the Music Trade only:
MUSIC SALES LIMITED
8/9 Frith Street, London W1V 5TZ, UK.

Photo Credits:
Front cover photograph: Steve Jennings/Corbis LGI
Back cover: Dennis Kleiman/Retna

Jay Blakesberg/Retna, Pg. 37
Larry Busacca/Retna, Pg. 35
Kevin Estrada/Retna, Pg. 20
Steve Granitz/Retna, Pg. 34
John Hughes/London Features, Pg. 31
Mick Hutson/Retna, Page 32
Steve Jennings/Corbis LGI, Pgs. 8 & 9
Dennis Kleiman/Retna,
Pgs. 3, 4 & 5, 7, 12, 14, 18, 20, 41, 42, 47

Patrick McMullan/London Features, Pg. 44
Eddie Malluk/Retna,
Pgs. 22, 29, 38 & 39, 43
BJ Papas/Retna, Pgs. 15, 23
John Popplewell/Retna, Pgs. 21, 26,
Michael A. Schreiber, Pgs. 27, 48
John Soares/Retna, Pg. 13
Kelly A. Swift/Retna
Pgs. 6, 10, 17, 19, 25, 30, 36, 40, 45

Color separations by Color 4 Graphics Inc.
Printed in the United States of America by Vicks Lithograph and Printing Corp.

OMNIBUS PRESS

Why is No Doubt one of the strangest bands to hit Number One in recent years? Well, they don't claim to have invented a revolutionary brand of music that is unique and all their own, although that's what it sounded like to the bulk of their new fans at the beginning of 1996. Most of America's young MTV-ites couldn't even recognize New Wave when they heard it in the opening riff of "Just a Girl," much less ska, the main influence on the band's rollicking sound. No Doubt's music is a mad and seamless mix of punk, heavy metal, ska, reggae, rock, pop, and the kitchen sink – and they're the first to proudly admit it.

Add to this the fact that they are never, ever, what they seem. Yet another pissed-off female songwriter with a quick-fix backup group riding the nineties wave of angry young women? Guess again: this foursome is a full-fledged band that has been together for almost a decade now – with the convoluted history to prove it – and Gwen Stefani is the furthest thing from a rock chick you're likely to find this side of VH-1.

Allright, but judging by the Tasmanian-devil-style show this wild-looking group puts on, they must at least lead the classic sex, drugs, and rock 'n' roll lifestyle we've all heard so much about. Right? Wrong – here you have a drug-free band who have confessed to giving away their beer ration while on tour since each of them rarely even indulges in a wee dram. And if you think that fabulous platinum bombshell of a lead singer is reveling in her new-found status as sexy pop icon, well, that's a whole 'nother story.

So what is the deal then? Well, it all starts in a land called Disney....

openthegate

The band was kickstarted in 1987 by Eric Stefani, his sister Gwen, and their Orange County Loara High School buddy John Spence. The trio shared a fondness for British ska bands and the romping rhythms of two-tone. One day Eric came home from school with an import copy of the Madness single "Baggy Trousers," and things were never quite the same – he may as well have tossed a time-bomb onto the floor of the Stefani living room. From that moment on, Gwen "worshipped" the band known by most young Americans solely for the cheerful "Our House" single. The brother and sister team's first public musical debut was at a school talent show where they performed the song "On My Radio" by yet another U.K. ska outfit, the Selecter.

Ska, the seminal musical style known today as a sort of pumped-up, speeded-up, kick-ass reggae, actually originated in Jamaica in the late fifties and early sixties when Jamaican artists added their own indigenous musical styles to American rhythm and blues. The rather odd fusion of the local sounds of Mento, Burru, and Calypso with the R&B Jamaicans heard over the radiowaves from the States soon broke into its own groove. The early sixties saw the official formation of the Skatalites who backed many up-and-coming Jamaican artists including a young up-and-comer named Bob Marley. Jamaican ska, perhaps a little too fast-paced for the sun, sand, and spliff lifestyle of the islands, soonafter metamorphosed into the laid-back sound of reggae, which has remained the signature soundtrack of the dreadlocked ones. Ska all but disappeared into the Jamaican sunset until it re-emerged in a very different scene: late seventies England. Ska took on the nick-name "two-tone" (and indeed the record label 2-Tone was founded) as bands blended the best of black and white musicians to form groups like Madness, the

English Beat, the Selecter, and the Specials. The two-tone ska movement in the U.K. was huge, and its roots as well as its outshoots were far-reaching. Madness, due largely to the MTV support of its "Our House" video, and the English Beat – also thanks to MTV's heavy rotation of its "Save It for Later" video – broke into the U.S. music scene briefly, but U.K. ska and two-tone outfits remained cult and college radio favorites for years Stateside. So-called "third generation" ska bands started forming in Southern California in the eighties, most notably bands like Fishbone, the Untouchables, and, a little later on, the Mighty Mighty Bosstones, Rancid, and Sublime. As seemed to be symptomatic of ska, these bands added their own flavor to the genre, with a little of the heavier, funkier sound of the Californian scene sneaking in to the mix.

But back to Anaheim in the eighties... John Spence was determined to be in a rock band, and was caught up in the wave of his friends Eric and Gwen's enthusiasm for ska, recognizing it as an easily emulated style of music for the novice. It was Spence whose catch-phrase was "no doubt," and so he, perhaps unintentionally, christened the band and was the front man, although Gwen shared his duties as vocalist. As she years later

told MTV VJ Kennedy for *SPIN* magazine, "John didn't really sing. He yelled and screamed and did back flips, and I was like his little sidekick." Nonetheless, his contagious stage bravado taught the rather reluctant Gwen a thing or two. The band's early gigs were local parties; the two singers were backed by Eric on keyboards and a revolving roster of other amateur musicians. As Gwen reminisced to *SPIN* in their November 1996 issue, "We sucked, but for some reason there was automatically this built-in following."

The threesome soon became a foursome with the addition of Tony Kanal, a junior to Gwen's status as senior at the high school who played bass in the school jazz band. Born in India, Tony was raised in England until being transplanted to Southern California just before entering his teen years, and it may be that his U.K. roots – the closest any of the band had come to the homeland of their beloved Madness – tipped the scales in his favor. Then again, he may just have been the best bass player who wanted the job. After but a few months, not only was he there to stay, he had become the band's manager as well. To top it off, he and Gwen began what was to be a seven year relationship, the end of which would inspire most of the songs on their 1996 Number One album.

so *high* **the** climb

No Doubt's early gigs were learning experiences, but never took on an aura of tedium – rather, they were outrageously energetic, kinetic affairs. The budding band rehearsed twice a week, on Thursdays and Sundays, and all chipped in for the studio rental fees. As Gwen told the No Doubt Official Web Page in the "The Hub Interview" in December of 1996, "I remember having to ask my dad for money every time. I remember John Spence having a plastic baggie full of pennies and counting them out every week. Remember we used to pay two dollars for a mic? We'd be like, 'Do we really have to get two mics? We could share.'" The spring and summer of 1987 saw them playing in venues like Fender's in Long Beach; Gino's, Roxy, and Whisky in Hollywood; and a fair share of house parties. It was then, right as the band was starting to gel and gain momentum, that a tragic event took place. In December of 1987, John Spence committed suicide by shooting himself in the head. "When your friend dies like that and it's so unexpected it's very traumatic," Gwen was to tell Axcess magazine in April/May 1996. "I think it taught us all a big lesson in how much one person can influence so many different people."

No Doubt did not disband, but carried on, enlisting the services of another vocalist to accompany Gwen in seventeen-year-old Alan Meade, whose brief tenure with the group ended before it had really begun when he left to become a husband and father. By this time Gwen had earned her stripes and gained enough confidence to take the reins as the one and only lead singer of the band.

It was 1988, and No Doubt practiced in a rehearsal complex in Anaheim where little soundproofed rooms with windows in the doors could be rented by the hour. Among the many local bands that also used the space was a heavy metal group called Rising, and its guitarist Tom Dumont did a peeping Tom routine through the window of No Doubt's room now and then. After several years in the competitive Orange County hard rock crowd, Dumont was becoming disillusioned. As he put it in No Doubt's official record company bio, "It was such an unhealthy scene. People weren't there for the music, they were there to wear tight spandex and get chicks." Dumont just had to get out, and quit Rising, only to discover a notice on the rehearsal complex bulletin board: No Doubt Looking for Guitarist. As he was to tell *Guitar World* magazine in their December 1996 issue, "When I played my first No Doubt show, which was a week after I had started rehearsing with them, we played in front of 600 or 700 people. Everybody was dancing and having a ton of fun. I felt like this great weight had been lifted, and music was fun again."

The band's local following continued to grow. Curious punters, perhaps a little weary of the over-serious poser attitude of the heavier bands' gigs, got into the atmosphere of No Doubt shows and became dedicated followers after their first exposure to the group. Here was a band that was actually, well, *fun* to see, and the lead singer – powerhouse vocals and all – was a girl who encouraged the growing number of females in the crowd to join in. Early shows were often "All Ages" affairs, and No Doubt found themselves on playbills with the likes of Fishbone, Urban Dance Squad, and Ziggy Marley and the Melody Makers. One notable gig was November 26, 1988, when No Doubt opened for the Red Hot Chili Peppers in the Multipurpose Room at Cal State, Long Beach. Indeed, Flea reportedly helped the band record their first demo. In 1989 Adrian Young, a regular member of the group's mosh pit for some time, actually joined his favorite band, allegedly playing drums for the very first time when he auditioned. Incredibly enough, the novice drummer has remained with the band ever since and is now known for his precision-pop style of playing.

get on the ball

What did the early No Doubt have in common when they all finally came together? Musically, not a lot, but it was this very diversity in influences and ideals that made the band unique. Tony Kanal cites Flea, the bass player for the Chili Peppers, along with fellow ska-esque band Fishbone, as inspirations, but the funk-loving bass player's main idol was the Artist Then Known as Prince. Tom Dumont would later tell *Guitar World* magazine in August of 1996, "Ever since I got my first Kiss record, I wanted to be a guy in a rock band," and has also listed Iron Maiden, Judas Priest, and Black Sabbath as mentors of sorts. Adrian Young's original musical leanings were in the Jimi Hendrix/seventies rock direction, but he also had a predilection for all things Gothic along with his fair share of Madness mania. Eric Stefani, the mastermind behind the band and the main songwriter, was in fact a visual artist with an excess of creativity on his hands; playing keyboards and composing were just a few of his outlets. Gwen's main influences? Her brother Eric, *The Sound of Music*, and Kermit the Frog.

This unlikely combination, brought together over the course of a good couple of years, was proving to be an irresistible concoction. No Doubt was known to locals as one of the most exciting live bands around. Tony Kanal later described the atmosphere to *Guitar World*, saying "I think what happened in the very late eighties and early nineties was that the whole ska scene and the punk scene kind of merged together, especially in California. It just became one cohesive scene… it was like this group of skater/alternative/what-ever-you-want-to-label-them-as kids going to shows." No Doubt took their opportunity to play in front of fairly diverse audiences as a challenge, and made their stage show as colorful, kinetic,

and wild as possible. On any given night Gwen might appear on stage wearing silk Oriental pajamas, her long dirty-blond hair in a tight bun; Tony in a doctor-scrub-blue jumpsuit; Tom with a mohawk hairdo; Eric in a suit and bow-tie; and Adrian shirtless. The group, in true ska style, embellished their live sound with a three-piece horn section, and on at least one occasion featured Gwen's sisters as dancers. "What we've become now is stuff that we taught ourselves and learned how to do," Gwen explained in the "Hub Interview." "It wasn't something, like, we just had. Our whole show, we used to practice hours and hours and hours on trying to be energetic inside the studio. It was all stuff that was really learned."

The band's reputation for true-blue spectacle-style entertainment, along with their ever-expanding mish-mash of musical styles, caught the eyes and ears of Tony Ferguson, an English A&R man with Madness roots of his own. Ferguson convinced industry big-wig Jimmy Iovine, whose name features in the stories of an eclectic list of artists including Trent Reznor and John Lennon, and who had just started up a new record label called Interscope, to check the scene out at a No Doubt gig one night in 1991. Iovine allegedly looked into his music business crystal ball and, after making the astonishingly accurate prediction that Gwen Stefani would be a Star with a capital "S" in five years time, signed No Doubt to Interscope Records.

behind castle walls

The songs that No Doubt had been writing, practicing, and performing for the last few years were finally to be recorded and released. The band had been playing quite consistently all over Southern California, juggling gigs with their college schedules at Cal State Fullerton. Tom, Eric, and Adrian had moved into "The Band House," formerly Eric and Gwen's grandparents' house, while Gwen and Tony still lived at home with their respective parents. It was now time to go into the studio full-time, and No Doubt recorded their debut album of the same name from October of 1991 to January of 1992 at A&R Studio in Hollywood. Joining the five official members of the band on the album were Eric Carpenter on saxophone, Don Hammerstedt on trumpet, and Alex Henderson on trombone. The album was dedicated to John Francis Spence.

No Doubt opens with a forty-four second long instrumental entitled "BND," and ends fourteen tracks later with the expanded vocal version of the same tune in the cheery, optimistic "Brand New Day." Gwen's unusual and expressive voice weaves its way through the album's veritable feast of musical flavors as she sings words penned by all and sundry. Although Eric was the main song-writer, when it came to lyrics the band's method was for all to chip in – they considered it part of the learning experience – and so Gwen found herself singing about her brother having his wisdom teeth pulled in "Ache."

If there is a track on this album that perhaps best encapsulates the spirit of the band, it is "Move On." From the heavy-metal guitar intro and solo, the manic punk/ska chanting of the lines "*You have to understand that when it comes to making MU-SIC / We meshed the styles of five alive and inter-twined and FUSED IT,*" to the song's reggae elements and a horn and drum segment surely inspired by Madness' "One Step Beyond," this tune pays homage to all of its members' musical inclinations. Credited to all five, the song has become an anthem of sorts with its "*Don't be afraid, let your feelings show*" sentiment; its theme is to keep moving and changing. As Gwen told the Official Web Page, "That's one song that's really lasted. We still play that every show, and it's still really powerful."

The catchy "Trapped in a Box," a song that began as a short poem Tom composed about how he felt when he watched too much TV (*Controlling my mind, what to eat, what to buy / Subliminal rules: how to live, how to die*) was chosen as the single. The video opens with a fat balding man slumped in a chair, a remote control in one hand and a beer in the other, staring at the tube, while all around him people speed through the room – life is passing him by. The majority of the video is shot in what looks to be one of the band members' bedrooms into which they have stuffed Adrian's drum kit, Eric's keyboards, and a TV on a white Roman pillar of a pedestal. The band pogo jumps around the tiny room whose walls are plastered with No Doubt artwork; perhaps due to the many small stages they've played in their time, they seem quite at home in such close quarters. Gwen wears a rather domestic-looking plaid sleeveless dress, flashing the camera a peak underneath to disclose a pair of men's boxer shorts. Her hair is its natural dark blonde, and she wears little make-up, but her antics and mannerisms are a clear indication of the Gwen we know today. A long-haired Tony sports his usual jumpsuit, Tom is in shorts and what appears to be a policeman's blue shirt, Eric's duds are cartoon-colorful, and Adrian sticks to the basics, hiding behind his drums in nothing but a pair of boxers. Signature No Doubt zaniness

abounds, with Tony brushing his teeth while still holding on to his bass. Mid-song, the scene switches to a huge white stage, and the band is done up in suits, bowties, and suspenders (the boxer-clad Adrian being the exception, of course), with Gwen looking vaguely Madonna-esque (from the "Material Girl" era) and the three-piece horn section in red and white candy stripes. Tony's dance partner is a stand-up bass, and Eric is captured doing his own version of the jig while playing an upright piano. The video also flashes to a darkened room filled with people gathered around Gwen's face on a TV screen, but it is the packed bedroom set that really seems to capture the band's close-knit sense of fun. After all, that's what music is all about, isn't it – a bit of fun?

sunpist

Unfortunately for No Doubt, the voice of grunge uttered a resounding No, and music that was fun was suddenly transformed into music that was frivolous, dishonest, and, worst of all, totally uncool. The sound of Seattle and its Sub Pop label was the sound of the moment, and the angst, disillusionment, and rage of the grunge movement had touched a chord with the country's youth: no one with any sense was in the mood to dance about with a smile on his or her face. With the unprecedented and unexpected multiplatinum success of Nirvana's *Nevermind* album – which knocked Michael Jackson off the top of the US charts in January 1992 – came a completely new nationwide take on popular music. Nirvana's Kurt Cobain became the reluctant spokesman for a generation's feelings of despair and discontent. And No Doubt's happy little debut album never saw the light of day.

Nonetheless, the band had taken a few semesters off from college to tour in support of their new-found state of band with label. They performed in front of new audiences in Las Vegas, Arizona, New Mexico, Colorado, and even Canada, as well as playing a much more extensive line-up of gigs in their home state. By the second half of 1992, No Doubt was on a full-time tour, and October and November saw them playing almost every night as they moved across the country through Texas, Louisiana, Florida, and on to the East Coast with shows in Massachusetts, Vermont, and Chicago. As Tony would later tell *Guitar World* magazine in their December 1996 issue, "That's not to say we were completely destitute and things were horrible, because since 1987 we've always – *always* – had a great following, especially on the West Coast. So we had that to keep us going the whole year, and we could always come home and do sold-out shows wherever we wanted."

One valuable lesson the band did seem to learn from the release of *No Doubt* was through the reactions of some of their die-hard fans to the CD; somehow, the No Doubt captured on disc was not quite up to snuff compared to the No Doubt fans went mad for at shows. The band decided that they needed to switch their focus from wild stage shows to the songs themselves, making them strong enough to stand on their own even without the mosh-pit-style excitement of a gig. The group resolved to not only write better songs, but to somehow capture and transfer their live energy onto their next recording.

Alas, after over two years had gone by the likelihood of a "next" No Doubt recording was growing smaller and smaller. The band had been touring quite consistently without record company support, although some months in 1993 and 1994 featured only one or two gigs and the band stuck to the West Coast. At the end of '94 Interscope finally gave the band the green light to record again, and what was to become the Number One multimillion-selling *Tragic Kingdom* album was recorded in no fewer than eleven different Californian studios and then shelved.

greener pastures

The members of No Doubt, meanwhile, had not been taking the lack of record company action lying down, and had been in the process of recording an albums-worth of songs in their Beacon Street garage. After all, ska and punk have had many good times together, and a little D.I.Y. never hurt anyone. Hence, the band's second release, entitled *The Beacon Street Collection* and on the band's own Beacon Street label, was out in early 1995. Gwen explained to *Circus* magazine (Volume 27, No. 5) that "We were really frustrated being a band and not being able to put music out." She confesses that the independent album was "definitely sneaky, and we didn't do it because we were allowed to. We did it because we needed to."

The band had been writing songs ever since the release of their eponymous debut, and, aside from their impatience, knew that only a choice few of the sixty or so songs they had penned would make it onto the next Interscope release; they thought the ten songs they recorded for *The Beacon Street Collection* deserved to be saved from disappearing into never-never land. The CD is now available for $10.00 through the No Doubt Official Web Page, and features some interesting tunes that concert-goers will remember from live shows. The CD cover artwork is also quite memorable: a sort of Phil Collins look-a-like swallowing a live fish along with the original "No Doubt" logo as on the first CD. One of the tracks, "Total Hate 95," is notable as it wasn't written by any of the current members of the band but rather by founding member John Spence and two others. This song also features a dub/rap segment courtesy of the late Brad Nowell of Sublime; he sings "*Long beat, Long Beach and it feels so fine / Rock this shit straight back to Anaheim.*" Nowell, along with the rest of the band, stopped by to hang out with No Doubt just as they were recording the song and improvised the verses. Yet another track entitled "Snakes" has since been given the dubious honor of appearing on the *Beavis and Butt-head Do America* soundtrack alongside the likes of Rancid, the Red Hot Chili Peppers, AC/DC, and, oddly enough, Englebert Humperdink. The song, written by Tony and Gwen, put the band's negative feelings about the record industry into words (*Hidden in the many trenches of a hopeless war / Those who were sold out by a corporate board*).

No Doubt underwent a dramatic change after the recording of *Tragic Kingdom* when Eric officially left the band to pursue a full-time career as an animator for the television show *The Simpsons*.

Although he plays piano and keyboards on the album, his interest in the band had been waning, and songwriting duties, in the past mainly Eric's domain, had fallen in the laps of the other members. It was a difficult, albeit challenging, event for the band to deal with, although they were supportive of his decision. As Tony later told *Circus* magazine (Volume 27, No. 5): "[Eric] stopped writing and it forced the rest of us to step up to bat. For us, it's really exciting because we'd never been songwriters before, writing music, where me and Gwen actually wrote a complete song. It's like there's so much more to go." Eric's creativity had fueled No Doubt from the onset, and it was almost as if he taught them all he could and then let them go on their own way. He reportedly relished songwriting and experimenting with music at home or in a studio far more than touring and performing. During the MTV "No Doubt: Here and Now" special Tony explained that Eric "just wasn't enjoying all the other things that came along with being in a band – which is understandable."

Gwen to this day credits her brother with putting her in her current position of stardom (to which she still attaches a how-the-hell-did-this-happen brand of disbelief). As she told *Axcess Magazine*, "I never really thought about being in a band. I mean, maybe when I watched *Donnie and Marie* I thought, 'God I wish I could be Marie,' but that was the closest I'd come." She told *Circus* magazine that Eric "was the one who got me into this. He was always pounding on the piano and forcing me to come into the living room and sing with him and stuff like that," while she was content "on the couch as a kid watching *The Brady Bunch*, really lazy with no goals and no ambition."

themagickingdom

Tragic Kingdom was saved from dying a lonely death on a dusty industry shelf largely due to the enthusiasm of Paul Palmer who was called in to mix the album. Palmer, fresh from mixing an album entitled *Sixteen Stone* for another due-to-be-huge band called Bush, co-owned (with Rob Kahane) a boutique label under the wing of Interscope Records called Trauma. The nurturing and attentive atmosphere of the new label was just what the doctor ordered for a band that had just about given up hope.

No Doubt's *Tragic Kingdom* was released in October of 1995, although it did not enter the Billboard charts until January of 1996. It was produced by Matthew Wilder, whose work on the album gave the band exactly the recorded sound they had been striving for over the years. "I learned a lot from working with Matthew, personally," Gwen noted in the as MTV "No Doubt: Here and Now" special. "Just learning how to record a record and use all the different technical things to make it sound like a lot of energy versus sounding like a demo." Eric Stefani is of course listed as one of the band, and longtime hornsters Phil Jordan (trumpet) and Gabe McNair (trombone and additional percussion) are credited as sort of junior members. No Doubt thanks all of their families on the sleeve notes, as well as "all of our neighbors on Beacon Street." The CD cover, which would become a very familiar sight to the record-store-frequenting public once 1996 was in full swing, features Gwen in red plastic proudly holding up a hole-ridden orange, rather like a twisted Vanna White. The rest of the band is pictured underneath a barren-looking orange tree, while giant flies descend. The term "Sunpist" turns up here and there, and the band pays homage to

its native land of Anaheim on the sleeve: its orange groves, shopping carts, highways, mountains, and Disneyland are all there.

Tom Dumont, during his interview with Evan Zelig backstage at U.C. Irvine's Bren Events Center on Halloween night 1996, explained his feelings about Disneyland, one of the inspirations behind the song and album title *Tragic Kingdom*. He recognizes that oftentimes creativity and business go hand in hand in our society, calling it "the balance of commercialism and art." He said that he feels that taking into account the corporate giant that Disney has become that "there is a lot of great, creative, artistic stuff that they are able to do within the framework of a business. I think it's inspiring in some ways." This way of thinking may be a bit new for someone for whom creativity and success – from a business and financial standpoint – have only recently come head to head.

The album is a manic amalgam of the many musical styles No Doubt likes to mix up – and what a mix it is. Listening to the fourteen tracks is a veritable rollercoaster, bumper car, tunnel of love, and Space Mountain of a ride. Gwen's inimitable voice alternately quivers and quakes, soars, purrs, and growls its way through the hour's worth of music. The signature blend of ska, reggae, heavy metal, melodic pop, and more all manages to come together to form an inventive and entertaining whole. Of course, the band, as pleased as they are with the album, have their token disappointment; it seems that the band was none too pleased with the outcome of "World Go 'Round" on the album and don't even play the song anymore, likening it to "a Budweiser commercial." As Adrian put it in "The Hub Interview," "It's a bunch of white guys playing bad

reggae." That aside, a few new pieces have been added to the puzzle this time around, most notably in the disco-informed dance tune "You Can Do It" and in the choked-up, tear-stained ballad "Don't Speak" which features a Spanish guitar solo. This song (*I really feel / I'm losing my best friend / I can't believe / This could be the end*) also introduces a common thread in the album's lyrical subjects: the end of Tony and Gwen's seven-year relationship, which was drawn out over the time frame of the album's creation.

Breaking up is, as they say, hard to do, but Gwen reportedly found it near-impossible and her struggle to accept Tony's decision is evident in many of the song's lyrics. As the grown-up version of a young girl whose future plans heavily featured the terms "wife" and "motherhood" with a distinct lack of "pop icon" or "rock star" sings in "Hey You": "*You're just like my Ken and Barbie doll / Your name will never change.*" Gwen addressed the issue of her relationship with Tony in *SPIN* magazine's June 1996 issue, stating that "Basically, I forced Tony to make out with me…. He didn't even like me and I made him kiss me. Then I forced him to go out with me for seven years." (She then went on to clear up the whole sex thing by advising her fans to "avoid having sex with anyone until you get married. It just brings too many complications.") Although both Tony and Gwen avow that they have managed to maintain a very close, caring friendship, it is certainly a bizarre situation. To play out how hurt you've been by the guy who dumped you in front of worshipping throngs of fans while that very guy takes part in the fun and games – even Alanis Morissette cannot lay claim to such public revenge. As Gwen snarls the lyrics to "Happy Now?" or "End It on This" (*I thought that we would last / Become a little family*), on stage

night after night, how does Tony feel? "It's fucking surreal," he told *SPIN* in their November 1996 issue. "I'm opening up my personal life to all these people. But I just can't get attached. I've got to separate myself from the music and the lyrics." Gwen is the first to come to Tony's defense, insisting that the words she sings are her point of view, and that there is always more than one side to any story.

The New Wave guitar opening of "Just a Girl," the album's first single, cut through the airwaves and had radioheads across the country pricking up their ears just in time to be introduced to the singular Voice of Gwen. Her sarcastic "'*I'm just a girl, all pretty and petite/So don't let me have any rights/Oh... I've had it up to here*" was alternately eetie-sweet-ie, poor little me, and in-your-face "enough already." It was also the perfect remedy for music fans who'd had more than their fair share of oh-so-serious female artists as of late. Having a father who despaired of you driving to your boyfriend's house late at night may not be the most earth-shattering and emotionally crippling occurrence of your life, but it sure is annoying. So why not sing a groovy song about it?

"Just a Girl" had its coming-out party (the band brought their own oranges) in January on MTV's Alternative Nation, with a jumpsuited Tony, Star Trek-shirted Tom, devil-horned Adrian, and mid-riff-baring Gwen all threatening to seriously devalue the set's oriental carpet as they gave their usual frenzied performance. The song snowballed its way through spring. As Tom Dumont told *Guitar World* magazine in their August 1996 issue "I consciously wanted to make a weird, jerky riff that sounded Devo- or B-52s-like. That single surprised the hell out of me. I mean, I always thought the song

was cool, but I never expected it to fly like it has." Fly it did, wings courtesy of MTV's devoted airing of the irresistible madcap "Just a Girl" video which managed to capture the band's live energy for the benefit of couch potatoes everywhere.

No Doubt's luck seemed to be on an upswing, and the band landed the opening slot for British mega-group Bush. Gwen, Tony, Tom, Adrian, and company joined Bush's 1996 Sixteen Stone Tour in Little Rock, Arkansas on Valentine's Day, and played half-hour sets of mostly *Tragic Kingdom* highlights before the main attraction hit the stage for nearly sixty nights before wrapping it all up in May with two sold-out shows at Denver's legendary Red Rocks Stadium. Bush's multiplatinum album, which seemed to comprise hit singles exclusively, was hot, and so was their lead singer Gavin Rossdale. As Gavin told MTV in January 1997, "Any band that has toured with us has without a doubt profited by the attention they get." It wasn't just No Doubt's music that was getting attention, however. Rumors abounded that Gavin and Gwen were more than tour-mates, a matter which is still up in the air. Both parties insist that they just like to hang out together, but then, they would, wouldn't they?

The Bush tour over, the band found themselves with yet another single under their belts in the hyperactive "Spiderweb." The video took the song's manic answering machine theme a step further into a whirling-dervish-style "attack of the killer phones" scenario. Gwen, plaid trousers and all, is at her kinetic best, and more than a few unsuspecting viewers surely took a step back from their TVs as she seemed to pop right out of the screen shouting out *"Sorry I'm not home right now / I'm walking into spiderwebs / So leave a message / And I'll call you back."*

The summer of '96 saw the band exporting the No Doubt experience to moshers around the world, playing to audiences in the U.K., Holland, Sweden, Denmark, Italy, Germany, and France, before hopping back over to their old West Coast U.S.A. stomping ground. September meant more than back to school for the growing legions of No Doubt-ites and "Gwennabies." The MTV 1996 Music Video Awards were on September 4th, and although the Smashing Pumpkins cleaned up trophy-wise, No Doubt kicked the games off by playing live from atop New York City's Radio City Music Hall marquee. The very next night the band gave another tip-top performance on *The Late Show with David Letterman*. Just as they were winding down a vigorous rendition of "Spiderweb," Gwen was suddenly inspired and ran over to the Desk of Dave, jumped on top of it, and crooned "I'll call you later" to the bemused host before turning to the audience with a "Yeah, right!" and proceeding to hop across his guests-only chairs and back to the stage. The song duly rounded off, Letterman came on stage, put his arm around the smirking lead singer and said, "Jump on the furniture at home? I'll bet you do!" The group then skipped the mainland, playing a gig in Hawaii on the way to the Australia/NewZealand/Indonesia/ Japan leg of their headlining tour.

spiders&snakes

Meanwhile, No Doubt, and, in particular, Gwen, had been attracting quite a bit of media attention. Web-sites were popping up left, right, and center. In the Prodigy on-line "chat" of March 27, 1996, in which all four members of the band participated, they discussed their stubborn refusal to give up over the past years. When asked what the best choices they'd ever made were, No Doubt replied, "Gwen says building the studio in our garage. Tom says to continue in the face of negative critics and to play a flying V." The band closed with the typically goofy send-off: "We are just going to keep touring this whole year and please come say high to us. Please don't stab your friends with forks, especially in the eyes."

Off-line, No Doubt articles were turning up in all manner of magazines. Gwen was featured in *Details'* July 1996 feature on "Violent Femmes: Eight Sisters with Voices and Looks to Die For" sporting a Versace chain-mail dress, but it was the November 1996 issue of *SPIN* magazine featuring Gwen and only Gwen on its cover which read "Riot Girlie – No Doubt Just Wanna Have Fun" that put the icing on the cake. *SPIN*'s following issue sparked letters praising the group ("Finally, a band that can express their pain without screaming" – Susan McGinley), bagging on Gwen (for "furthering the female stereotype" that the likes of Liz Phair and Tori Amos "strove so long to break" – Amy Boytz), and, surely to the guys in the band's satisfaction, complaining that "Gwen Stefani is really cool, but No Doubt is a group: They all deserved to be on your cover" – Adina Jaeger.

The band, in true take-it-with-a-pinch-of-salt style and their usual dose of upfront attitude, decided to confront the situation of Gwen overshadowing the band in the video for their third single, "Don't Speak." Cut in to a performance

set perhaps meant to represent their Beacon Street garage are live shots from the band's own headlining tour, but it is the staged scenes showing the rest of the band becoming ever-more frustrated as they are escorted out of photo shoots and Gwen is guided into the spotlight that illustrate the problem. The video seemed to do the cathartic trick, and the other bandmembers of course realized all along that lead singers in general, especially if they are attractive women in otherwise all-male bands, inevitably become the focus of attention.

The band's fourth video in support of their fourth single, "Excuse Me Mr.," addresses the issue in a much less serious

manner, as an overly-aggressive Gwen hogs the camera. The band do get a bit of sweet and silly revenge by tying the diva to railroad tracks – Tony even rubs his hands together in glee as the steaming train approaches, but it's all in fun and ends happily ever after.

As Tony told MTV News the week of January 17, 1997, "That whole situation was something that we dealt with for a year but we're kinda past it at this point. We've kinda like moved away from it, and we're concentrating on the future, and things that are important to us right now." And, let's face it, Gwen has that indefinable quality that true stars seem to unconsciously possess. "When Gwen sings she's just incredibly gripping and fascinating to watch," Tom Dumont is quoted as saying in the Trauma/Interscope Records Official No Doubt Bio. "There's something magical about her."

A year's worth of big-time touring has taken its toll at times: Gwen broke her foot in an overly manic stage jump, and was advised by a doctor not to speak for one full week at one point after reportedly straining her vocal cords. Adrian misses his girlfriend while he's on the road, and never seems to have time for his favorite pastime, hitting the golf course for a good eighteen holes. Tom hasn't hung out with a lot of his friends in a long time, and has been known to hark back to the joys of playing small Orange County gigs. And Gwen and Tony are, no matter what they may say, still two ex-lovers who spend more time together than most happily married couples.

No, it can't all be fun and games, and one inevitable bummer that comes along with multiplatinum success – especially after almost a decade of enjoying a small but dedicated cult following – is the cry of "Sell-out!" The music business is a funny, fickle industry. When you're relatively unknown you somehow haven't compromised your art – although no one would know this as no one has the opportunity to hear it – and when you finally get that precious record deal and MTV video and lots of people get to hear your music and you're playing to crowds every night, you've sacrificed your integrity and are only in it for the money. Which you haven't seen yet. Add to all of this the universal fact that no one likes a winner and jealousy is the best policy. So, how has No Doubt dealt with the negativity that has come their way? As Tom told Axcess magazine, "99% of musicians, whether they are telling the truth or not, want to make a living playing music. It's not about selling out. It's about having a little fun for a while and not having to work another job and getting to play music all day long, every day. It's really satisfying." After all, as Gwen told MTV in January 1997, "If you let people bring you down and bring your confidence level down, then you're just gonna disappoint people that are into you." Perhaps foreseeing future criticism, the cover of the *Tragic Kingdom* CD features, in the band's usual self-deprecating sense of humor, the logo "Bought and Sold Out in U.S.A."

No Doubt is indeed a band that takes a positive approach to the downside of things, and on January 11, 1997, they and a few fellow musicians confronted a much more serious problem that too often affects the music industry. "Enough Already," a benefit concert featuring Pennywise, the Vandals, the Ziggens, and the Voodoo Glowskulls, as well as No Doubt, was held at the Hollywood Palladium to raise money for Jakob, the son of Sublime's Brad Nowell who died of a heroin overdose, and for the Musician's Assistance Program.

happy now?

All in all, No Doubt seems to be grappling with the inherent difficulties of "sudden success" and all of the attention it brings with aplomb; they do not bemoan the problems that fame can bring like some artists, but rather take them in stride while remaining appreciative of its rewards. They are scheduled to perform at the 1997 Grammy Awards on February 26, and seem to be more excited about playing live than about the two awards they've been nominated for: Best Rock Album and Best New Artist. As Tony told MTV News, "We're gonna have a good time. It is gonna be a black tie affair, but our parents are going and our parents are getting into the moshing, they'll probably get a pit going." Playing their music live is the absolute motivation behind No Doubt, and is what has kept them going for the past decade. In April of 1997 they look forward to doing what they love best as they embark on another headlining U.S. Tour. They've also written quite a few new tunes, but when Trauma will be able to rope them in and harness their energy in a studio again is anybody's guess.

The band's overall feeling about their newfound position as Band of the Moment remains one of surprised satisfaction. In the Spring of 1996 Tony told *Axcess* magazine, "We're just so happy that people even want to take notice of us after all these years. We went to New York to do MTV and we were there on the set and Gwen and I just looked at each other and said, 'I can't believe we're doing this right now. I can't believe we're here.' It's really incredible." In the summer Gwen commented via cell phone from the No Doubt tour bus to the *Bucks County Courier Times* (August 21, 1996) "It's weird, isn't it? For years I never really thought we would get anywhere, but now we've finally gotten somewhere. It's an unreal feeling. This validates nine years of hard work." Some five months and five million album sales later, she told MTV's *Week in Rock* of January 17, 1997, "It's reached way, way higher than we ever thought it would go, we didn't even think the record would come out, let alone go to Number One. Which is just ridiculous, you know… hello? It's crazy."

Crazy? Maybe, but one thing's for certain – the strange and wonderful world of No Doubt has only just swung open the gates to its kingdom, and for most of us, the ride has just begun.

THE END

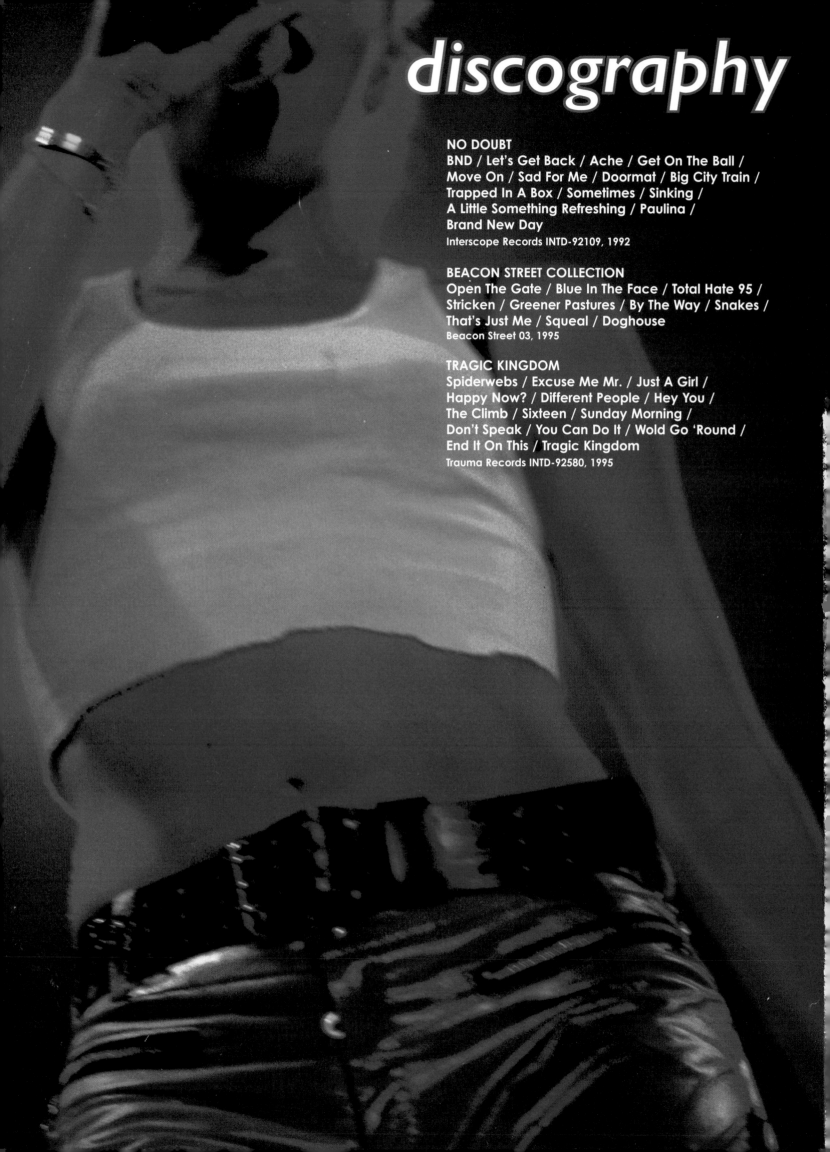

discography

NO DOUBT
BND / Let's Get Back / Ache / Get On The Ball /
Move On / Sad For Me / Doormat / Big City Train /
Trapped In A Box / Sometimes / Sinking /
A Little Something Refreshing / Paulina /
Brand New Day
Interscope Records INTD-92109, 1992

BEACON STREET COLLECTION
Open The Gate / Blue In The Face / Total Hate 95 /
Stricken / Greener Pastures / By The Way / Snakes /
That's Just Me / Squeal / Doghouse
Beacon Street 03, 1995

TRAGIC KINGDOM
Spiderwebs / Excuse Me Mr. / Just A Girl /
Happy Now? / Different People / Hey You /
The Climb / Sixteen / Sunday Morning /
Don't Speak / You Can Do It / Wold Go 'Round /
End It On This / Tragic Kingdom
Trauma Records INTD-92580, 1995